W9-CIB-120

Looking at . . . Spinosaurus

A Dinosaur from the CRETACEOUS Period

Weekly Reader® BOOKS

Published by arrangement with Gareth Stevens, Inc.
Newfield Publications is a federally registered trademark
of Newfield Publications, Inc. Weekly Reader is a federally
registered trademark of Weekly Reader Corporation.

Library of Congress Cataloging-in-Publication Data available upon request from publisher.
Fax: (414) 225-0377 for the attention of the Publishing Records Department.

ISBN 0-8368-1349-9

This North American edition first published in 1995 by
Gareth Stevens Publishing
1555 North RiverCenter Drive, Suite 201
Milwaukee, Wisconsin 53212 USA

Consultant: Dr. David Norman, Director of the Sedgwick Museum of Geology,
University of Cambridge, England.

Additional artwork by Clare Herronneau.

Printed in the United States of America

Weekly Reader Books Presents

Looking at . . . Spinosaurus

A Dinosaur from the CRETACEOUS Period

by Tamara Green

Illustrated by Tony Gibbons

Gareth Stevens Publishing
MILWAUKEE

Contents

Introducing Spinosaurus

A giant meat-eater, **Spinosaurus** (SPINE-OH-SAW-RUS) was a fierce, nasty-looking monster that roamed what is now northern Africa about 100 million years ago — during what scientists call Cretaceous times.

It relied on its size and terrible, crocodilelike jaws for frightening a victim, but could still plan an ambush to catch unfortunate prey.

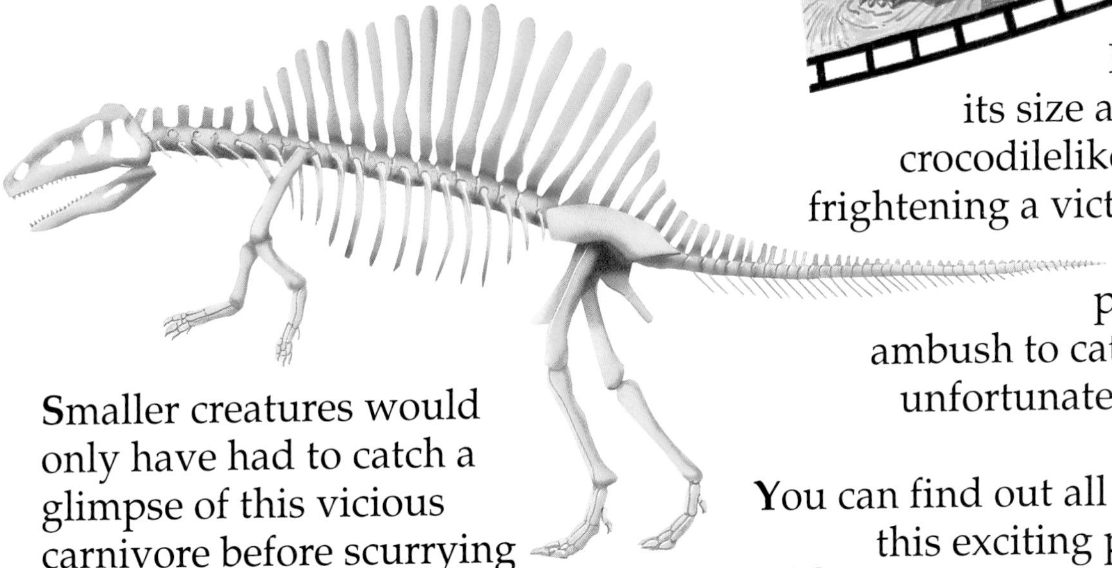

Smaller creatures would only have had to catch a glimpse of this vicious carnivore before scurrying away for their lives.

Although the largest of the dinosaurs discovered so far that have sails on their backs, **Spinosaurus** was probably not very intelligent.

You can find out all about this exciting prehistoric monster — one of the last that existed before dinosaurs became extinct — on the pages that follow.

Some of us are vegetarians and never eat meat. Dinosaurs that were herbivores also ate only plant food. But some of us, like the boy in this picture, dwarfed by the giant carnivore beside him, enjoy the meat in a hamburger.

Spinosaurus was heavy, too. Scientists think it may even have weighed as much as sixty men.

Spinosaurus, as you can see, was many times taller than a human being is today. In fact, it was so enormous it may even have eaten the equivalent of one hundred quarter-pounders every single day to satisfy its fantastic appetite!

In many respects, **Spinosaurus** was just like most other large carnivores, with massive jaws made for chewing great chunks of raw flesh. But there was one big difference. **Spinosaurus** also carried a huge sail-like structure on its back. This made it even larger and bulkier. At its central point, the sail alone was taller than you are.

What a terrifying beast it must have been!

Giant meat-eater

Spinosaurus was given its name — meaning "spine lizard" — by the German paleontologist W. Ernst Stromer von Rechenbach. He first discovered this dinosaur in Egypt, in northern Africa, in 1915. Unfortunately, these remains somehow got lost many years later during World War II. To this day, no one has found them. But, luckily, other **Spinosaurus** bones have since been discovered in Niger, another country in northern Africa. And perhaps others will be found in the future.

Huge, spined

About 40 feet (12 meters) long from the end of its jaws to the tip of its tail — that's more than the length of a city bus — **Spinosaurus** must have been one of the most feared creatures of Late Cretaceous times.

The most obvious thing about **Spinosaurus**'s skeleton was the large structure on its back. Inside this structure was a long row of tall spines. The largest spines, at the center, were 6 feet (1.8 m) tall.

Narrower in the middle than at the top end, the spines you can see in this skeletal reconstruction were covered by skin and formed a sort of sail that ran all the way along **Spinosaurus**'s back.

This sail probably helped **Spinosaurus** control its body temperature.

skeleton

Two strong, pillarlike legs supported **Spinosaurus**'s weight. Its feet ended in three sharp claws. There was also an additional smaller toe that was weak and seems to have had no special purpose. Its larger claws must have come in useful for holding down victims as they struggled to escape from such a vicious predator.

Spinosaurus's forelimbs were short but very powerful. They were ideal for grabbing at any creature destined to be its prey.

Its skull was very much like that of other large carnivorous dinosaurs, but the teeth were straighter than those of most other prehistoric meat-eaters. However, they were still as sharp as steak knives!

Spinosaurus's tail was long, broad, and powerful. It might even at times have been used to knock out a victim with a strong blow — if, for example, **Spinosaurus** attacked another dinosaur for food.

Portrait of a monster

In his book, *The Lost World*, the famous British writer Sir Arthur Conan Doyle (who also wrote about the great detective, Sherlock Holmes) pits his hero, Ed Malone, against a beast as awesome as **Tyrannosaurus rex** (TIE-RAN-OH-SAW-RUS RECKS) or **Spinosaurus** must have been. Just imagine his terror as he suddenly spies the monster:

His ferocious cry and the horrible energy of his pursuit both assured me that this was one of the great flesh-eating dinosaurs, the most terrible beasts which have ever walked this earth. As the huge brute loped along, it dropped upon its fore-paws and brought its nose to the ground every twenty yards or so. It was smelling out my trail... Up to then he had hunted by scent, and his movement was slow. But he had actually seen me as I started to run. From then onwards he had hunted by sight. Now, as he came round the curve, he was springing in great bounds... The moonlight shone upon his huge, projecting eyes, the rows of enormous teeth in his open mouth, and the gleaming fringe of claws upon his short, powerful forearms. With a scream of terror I turned and rushed wildly down the path. Behind me the thick, gasping breathing of the creature sounded louder and louder. His heavy footfall was beside me. Every instant I expected to feel his grip upon my back.

How would *you* feel if you suddenly realized that a **Spinosaurus** was slowly creeping up on *you*? It's lucky that Conan Doyle's story is pure fantasy — because, of course, humans had not yet evolved at the time of the dinosaurs.

Super-sail

Rising from **Spinosaurus**'s back was an enormous and curious structure. It was made up of several giant spines covered with skin.

Another African dinosaur — **Ouranosaurus** (OO-RAN-OH-SAW-RUS) — had a "sail" like this, too, but it was smaller. This has led scientists to assume that the sail might have had some special purpose — perhaps to help these dinosaurs survive in the climate of Cretaceous Africa.

In the middle of the day, for instance, **Spinosaurus** might have stood with its back to the sun, as you can see in the picture on the left. This position prevented the sail from absorbing the sun's warmth so **Spinosaurus** would not overheat. If, by chance, it did get too hot, **Spinosaurus** could also have taken a dip and submerged its sail a few times in water to cool down.

But in the early morning, even in warm Cretaceous times, temperatures were probably not as high as later in the day. It may even have been chilly for **Spinosaurus** at dawn. So perhaps, then, **Spinosaurus** stood with its sail facing the sun and absorbed what warmth it could, as shown in the illustration below.

An alternative theory, however, is that sails of this kind may have been a way for the male to attract a female. Perhaps a male **Spinosaurus** had a larger and more colorful sail than the female had.

No one knows for certain. Most scientists, however, think temperature control was the most likely purpose of that super-sail.

Out for the kill

Aegyptosaurus (EE-JIP-TOE-SAW-RUS) stretched its long neck up to the branches of a tall tree and crunched into the leaves. They were not as juicy as anticipated, however, perhaps because the extreme heat had dried them out. It was approaching noon, and the North African sun was beating down over what is now Egypt.

The large herbivore was grateful, however, for the shelter offered by the thick canopy of vegetation. Otherwise, it might not have been able to tolerate these extreme temperatures. It was looking forward to a refreshing drink at a nearby pool. It might even paddle a little, as it sometimes did, in the inviting stream as a way of cooling down.

Just as the **Aegyptosaurus** reached the water's edge, there was a deafening roar. **Spinosaurus** — about the same length as the herbivore but much bulkier and, of course, a meat-eater — was out for the kill.

Spinosaurus's jaws were dripping with saliva at the prospect of a huge feast.

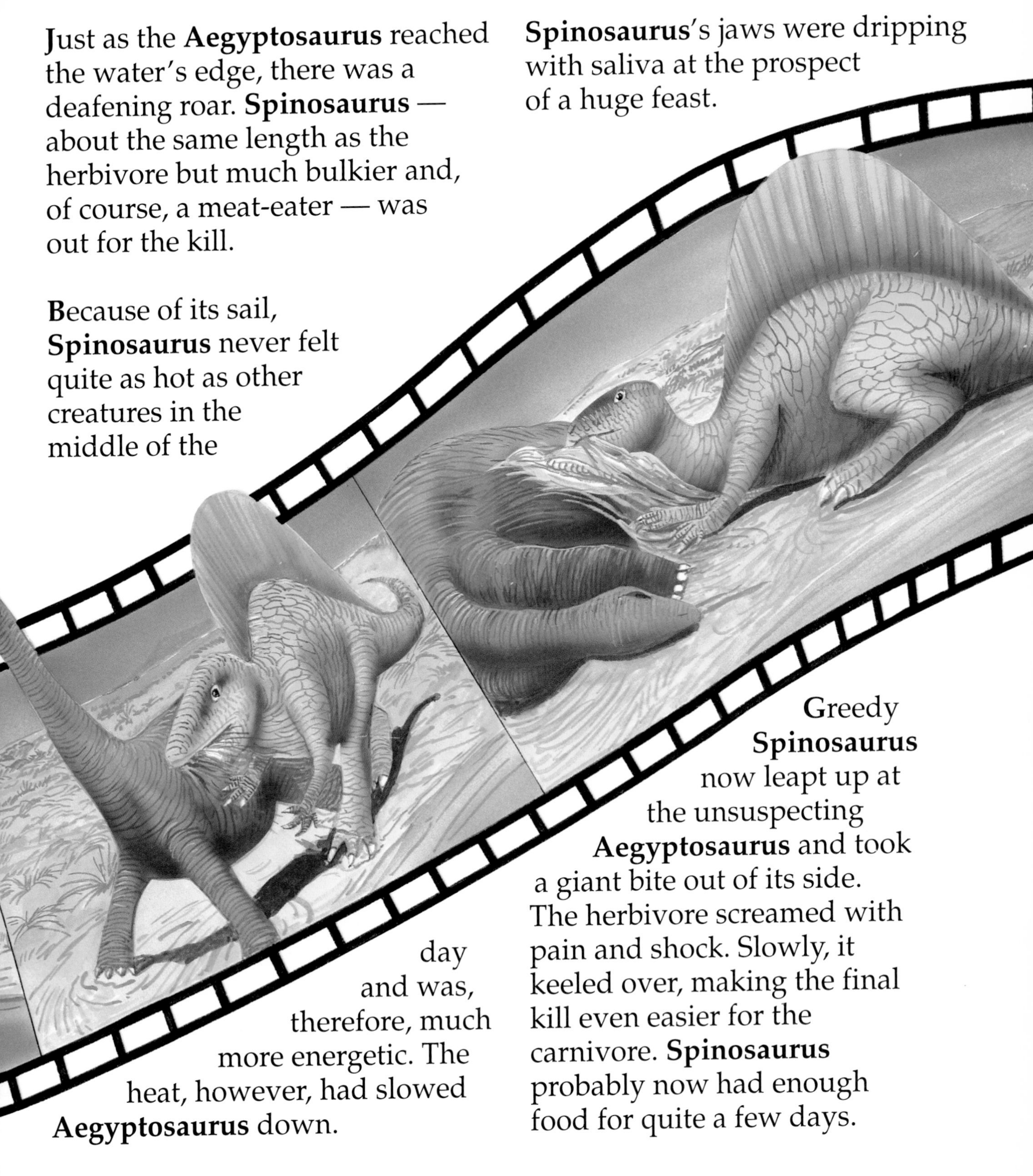

Because of its sail, **Spinosaurus** never felt quite as hot as other creatures in the middle of the day and was, therefore, much more energetic. The heat, however, had slowed **Aegyptosaurus** down.

Greedy **Spinosaurus** now leapt up at the unsuspecting **Aegyptosaurus** and took a giant bite out of its side. The herbivore screamed with pain and shock. Slowly, it keeled over, making the final kill even easier for the carnivore. **Spinosaurus** probably now had enough food for quite a few days.

The five dinosaur senses

Human beings have five senses: sight, smell, hearing, touch, and taste. And so did the dinosaurs.

Some of today's animals do not see in color. But scientists think dinosaurs did have color vision, just as you do. How far and how much they saw depended on where their eyes were positioned on their heads. If the eyes were at the very sides of the dinosaur's head — as they were on **Gallimimus** (GAL-EE-MIME-US), shown here to the far left — it could easily have caught sight of any predator creeping up from behind.

But dinosaurs probably did not have a good sense of touch, since their skin was generally thick and leathery. So even a small dinosaur like **Protoceratops** (PRO-TOE-SER-A-TOPS), for example, would not have responded much if you had been around to touch it.

Dinosaurs did not have ears that look like yours, but they did have the ability to hear. Scientists have found a spot in some skulls that may have been an eardrum. And, of course, if they could roar — like the **Parasaurolophus** (PARA-SAUR-OH-LOAF-US) above — as a warning or threat, then other dinosaurs must have been able to hear them.

Dinosaurs almost certainly had a good sense of taste. Carnivores like **Tyrannosaurus rex** (TIE-RAN-OH-SAW-RUS RECKS), below, would salivate over the raw meat they devoured in great chunks. Herbivores would chomp on delicious meals of foliage, berries, and other plant food.

Most carnivores, such as **Spinosaurus**, shown on the left, also had a very good sense of smell. They could easily sniff out a victim that was far away. Scientists know this because of the large nasal openings found in their fossilized skulls.

Dinosaur extinction

Many scientists think dinosaurs died out 65 million years ago when a large comet hit Earth. This is because they have found a lot of iridium in rocks dating from that time. And iridium is much more common elsewhere in the universe than on our planet.

The comet's crash caused a lot of damage to life on Earth, creating huge dust clouds that blocked out light and heat from the sun for a long time. Many plants and animals died as a result of this impact and its aftereffects.

Spinosaurus data

Imagine that you could travel back in time to 80 million years ago, and that you could explore northern Africa of that time. You would have had to beware: **Spinosaurus** might have attacked at any moment! It never tasted humans, of course, because humankind had not yet evolved. But maybe it would have enjoyed the flavor of our flesh. Luckily, you would have been able to spot a **Spinosaurus** right away.

But there would have been no time to lose! Once **Spinosaurus** caught the whiff of human flesh, it would have been likely to attack. How much safer you are in present-day times!

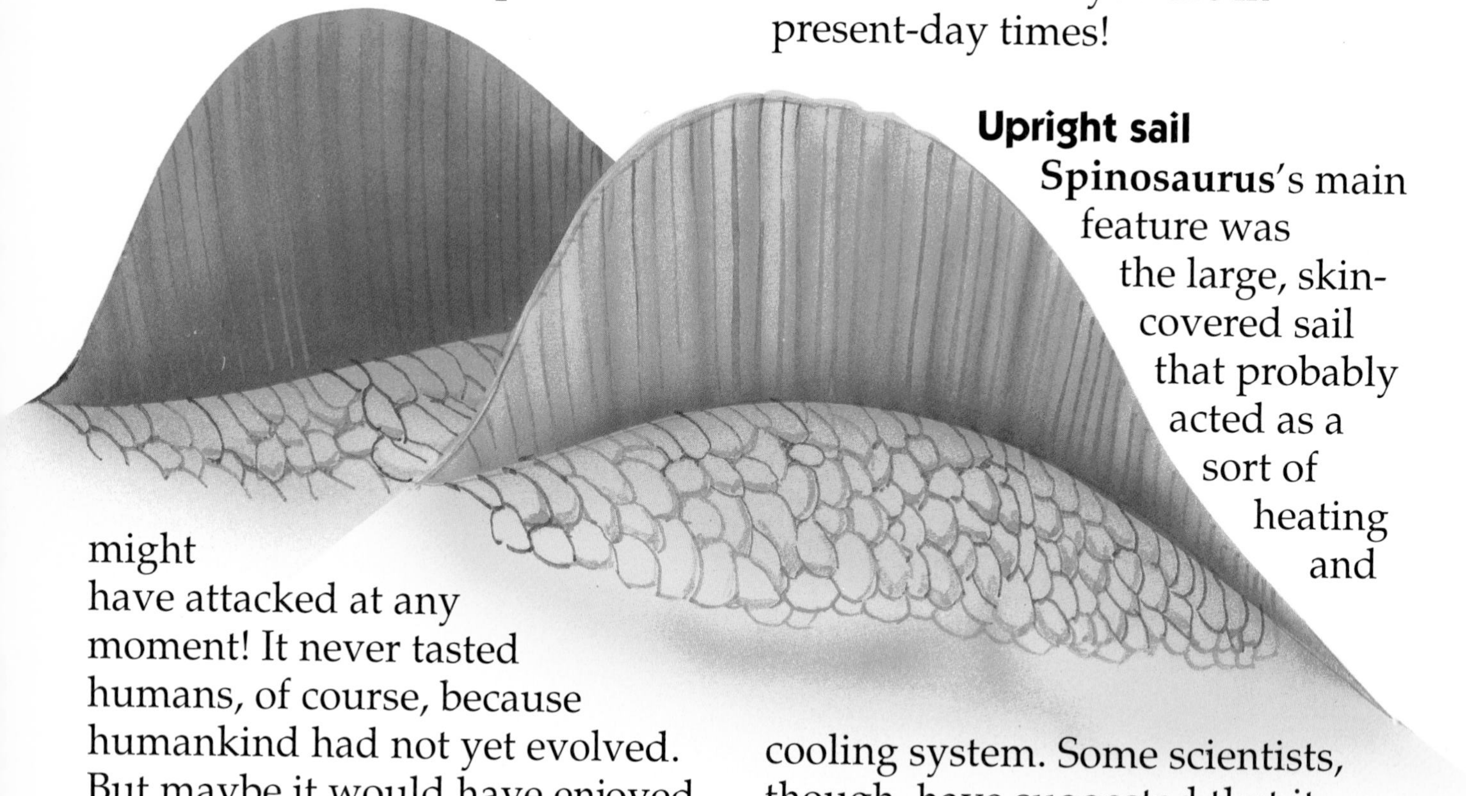

Upright sail

Spinosaurus's main feature was the large, skin-covered sail that probably acted as a sort of heating and cooling system. Some scientists, though, have suggested that it might have been more colorful in the males, and that it was perhaps some sort of mating display.

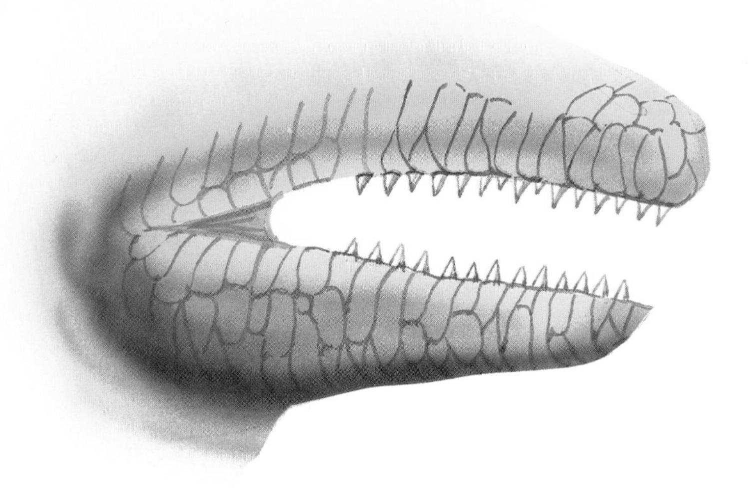

Clawed hands

Its short arms, ending in four clawed fingers, were useful, too, for stabbing and grasping.

Crocodile jaws

Spinosaurus was also easily recognizable because of its fierce-looking jaws, operated by strong muscles that helped it shut tight on prey. One bite and a victim would probably have been mortally wounded. Then, it would have provided one or more tasty meals for this carnivore.

Straight teeth

Unlike most carnivores, **Spinosaurus** had straight teeth. But they were as sharp as the curved teeth of beasts such as **Allosaurus** (AL-OH-SAW-RUS) or **Tyrannosaurus rex**.

Pillarlike legs

Spinosaurus's legs were so heavy that it might sometimes have killed small prey simply by stepping on them. Its clawed toes were also ideal for holding down struggling victims.

Mighty tail

And if those dreadful jaws and claws were not enough, **Spinosaurus** also had a strong, thick tail, powerful enough to give a nasty whack to a victim.

Spinosaurus (**1**), as we have seen, probably put that large sail to good use either to control its body temperature, so that it did not get too hot or too cold, or perhaps as a form of mating display. But it was not the only prehistoric creature to have had a structure of this kind rising from its back.

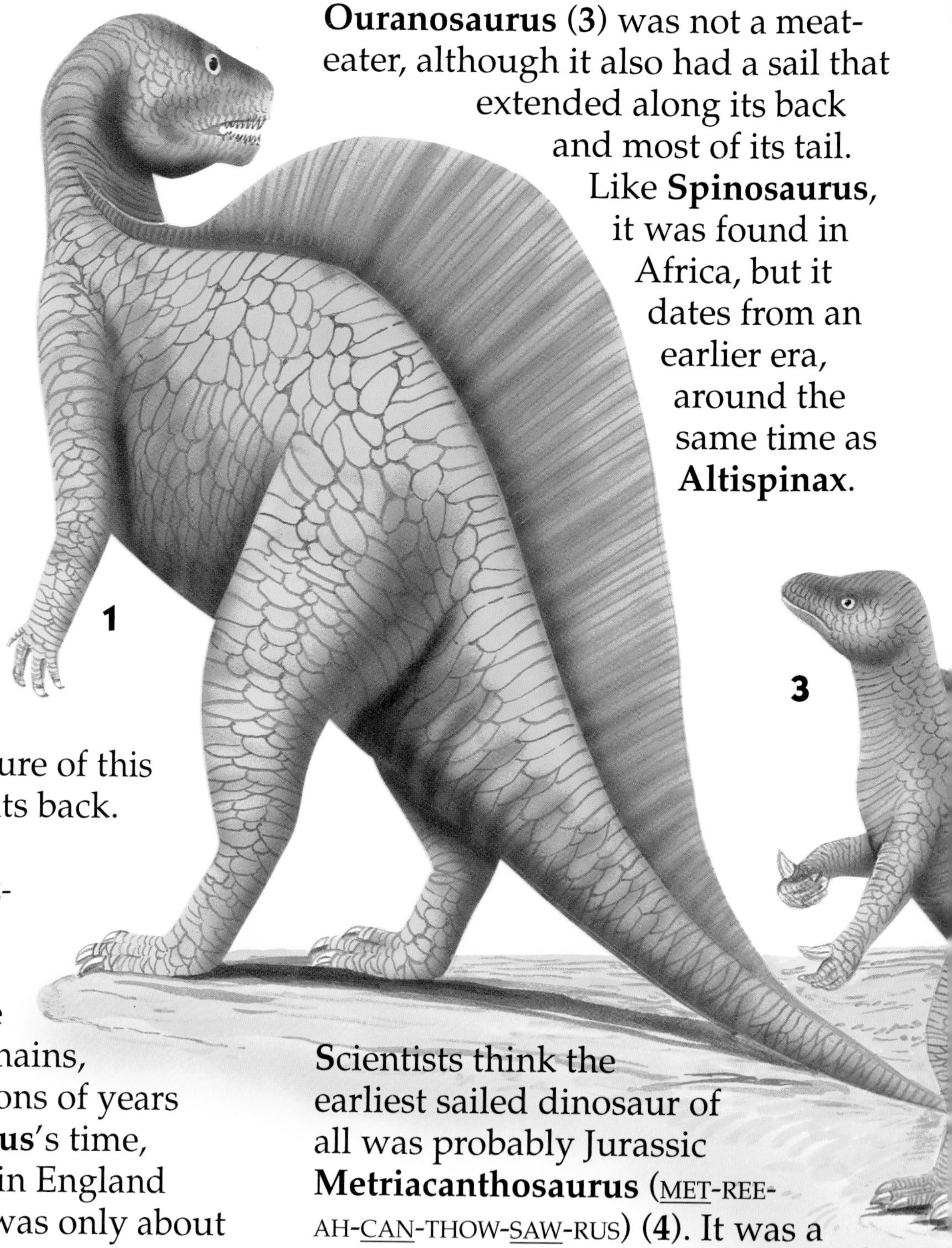

Ouranosaurus (**3**) was not a meat-eater, although it also had a sail that extended along its back and most of its tail. Like **Spinosaurus**, it was found in Africa, but it dates from an earlier era, around the same time as **Altispinax**.

1

3

Altispinax (AL-TEE-SPINE-ACKS) (**2**), for example, was another carnivore with a sail. Its remains, dating from millions of years before **Spinosaurus**'s time, have been found in England and Germany. It was only about half as long as **Spinosaurus**, but no doubt very fierce when hungry for its next meal.

Scientists think the earliest sailed dinosaur of all was probably Jurassic **Metriacanthosaurus** (MET-REE-AH-CAN-THOW-SAW-RUS) (**4**). It was a 26-foot (8-m)-long predator with skin-covered spines all along its back.

More creatures with sails

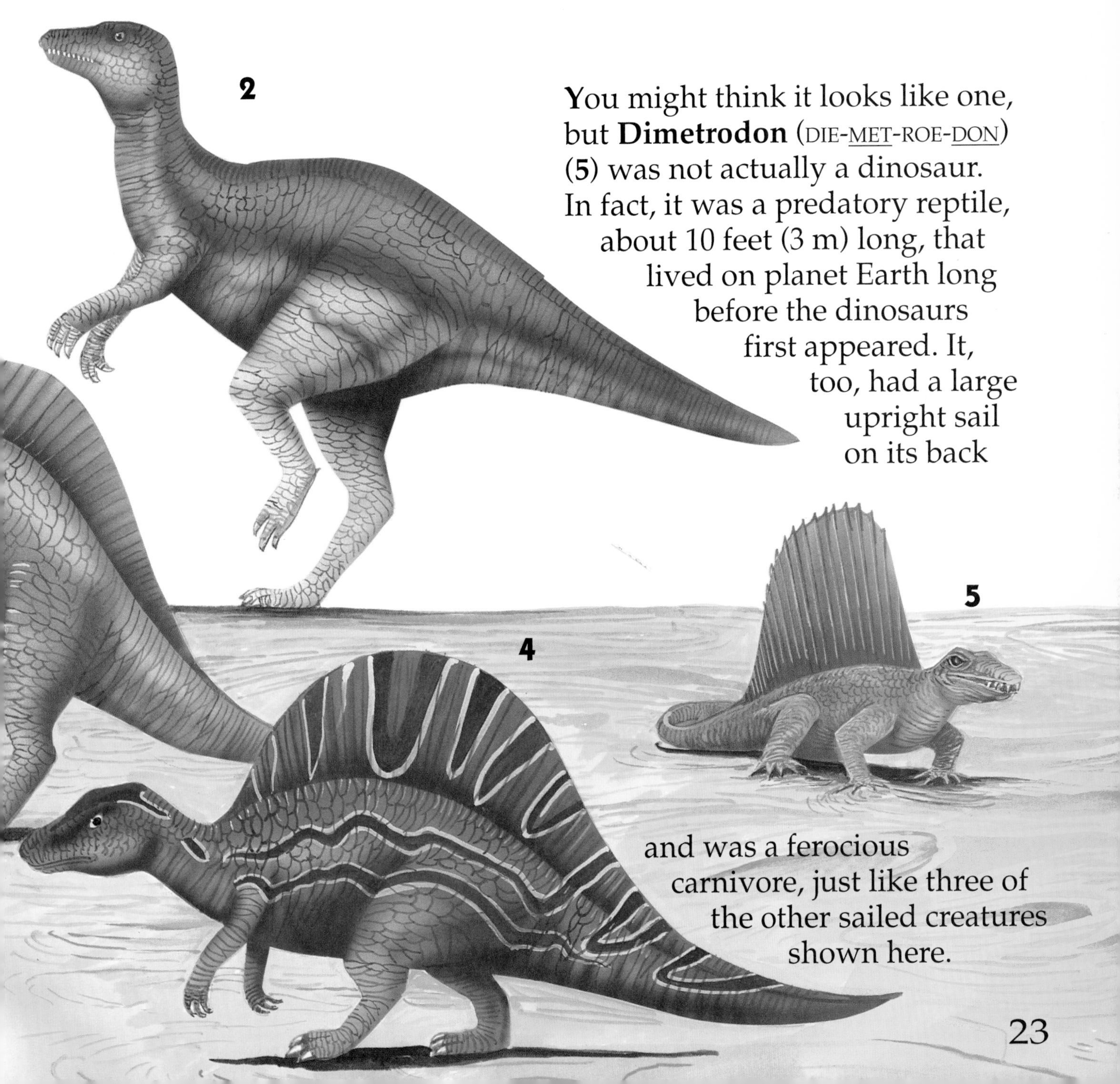

You might think it looks like one, but **Dimetrodon** (DIE-<u>MET</u>-ROE-<u>DON</u>) (**5**) was not actually a dinosaur. In fact, it was a predatory reptile, about 10 feet (3 m) long, that lived on planet Earth long before the dinosaurs first appeared. It, too, had a large upright sail on its back

and was a ferocious carnivore, just like three of the other sailed creatures shown here.

GLOSSARY

carnivores — meat-eating animals.

evolve — to change shape or develop gradually over a long period of time.

extinction — the dying out of all members of a plant or animal species.

foliage — a cluster or mix of leaves, flowers, and branches.

iridium — a silvery white, hard metallic element.

paleontologists — scientists who study the remains of plants and animals that lived millions of years ago.

predators — animals that kill other animals for food.

prey — animals that are killed by other animals for food.

remains — a skeleton, bones, or dead body.

INDEX